2019 CA

JANUARY

M	T	W	T	F	S	S
	1	2	3	4	5	6
7	8	9	10	11	12	13
14	15	16	17	18	19	20
21	22	23	24	25	26	27
28	29	30	31			

FE

M	T	W	T	F	S	S
				1	2	3
4	5	6	7	8	9	10
11	12	13	14	15	16	17
18	19	20	21	22	23	24
25	26	27	28			

M	T	W	T	F	S	S
				1	2	3
4	5	6	7	8	9	10
11	12	13	14	15	16	17
18	19	20	21	22	23	24
25	26	27	28	29	30	31

APRIL

M	T	W	T	F	S	S
1	2	3	4	5	6	7
8	9	10	11	12	13	14
15	16	17	18	19	20	21
22	23	24	25	26	27	28
29	30					

MAY

M	T	W	T	F	S	S
		1	2	3	4	5
6	7	8	9	10	11	12
13	14	15	16	17	18	19
20	21	22	23	24	25	26
27	28	29	30	31		

JUNE

M	T	W	T	F	S	S
					1	2
3	4	5	6	7	8	9
10	11	12	13	14	15	16
17	18	19	20	21	22	23
24	25	26	27	28	29	30

JULY

M	T	W	T	F	S	S
1	2	3	4	5	6	7
8	9	10	11	12	13	14
15	16	17	18	19	20	21
22	23	24	25	26	27	28
29	30	31				

AUGUST

M	T	W	T	F	S	S
			1	2	3	4
5	6	7	8	9	10	11
12	13	14	15	16	17	18
19	20	21	22	23	24	25
26	27	28	29	30	31	

SEPTEMBER

M	T	W	T	F	S	S
						1
2	3	4	5	6	7	8
9	10	11	12	13	14	15
16	17	18	19	20	21	22
23	24	25	26	27	28	29
30						

OCTOBER

M	T	W	T	F	S	S
	1	2	3	4	5	6
7	8	9	10	11	12	13
14	15	16	17	18	19	20
21	22	23	24	25	26	27
28	29	30	31			

NOVEMBER

M	T	W	T	F	S	S
				1	2	3
4	5	6	7	8	9	10
11	12	13	14	15	16	17
18	19	20	21	22	23	24
25	26	27	28	29	30	

DECEMBER

M	T	W	T	F	S	S
						1
2	3	4	5	6	7	8
9	10	11	12	13	14	15
16	17	18	19	20	21	22
23	24	25	26	27	28	29
30	31					

NOTES

December

Week 1

12/31/18 to 01/06/19

○ 31. MONDAY

○ 1. TUESDAY

○ 2. WEDNESDAY

○ 3. THURSDAY

○ 4. FRIDAY

○ 5. SATURDAY / 6. SUNDAY

NOTES

January

Week 2

01/07/19 to 01/13/19

○ 7. MONDAY

○ 8. TUESDAY

○ 9. WEDNESDAY

○ 10. THURSDAY

○ 11. FRIDAY

○ 12. SATURDAY / 13. SUNDAY

NOTES

January

Week 3

01/14/19 to 01/20/19

- ○ 14. MONDAY
- ○ 15. TUESDAY
- ○ 16. WEDNESDAY
- ○ 17. THURSDAY
- ○ 18. FRIDAY
- ○ 19. SATURDAY / 20. SUNDAY

NOTES

January

Week 4

01/21/19 to 01/27/19

○ 21. MONDAY

○ 22. TUESDAY

○ 23. WEDNESDAY

○ 24. THURSDAY

○ 25. FRIDAY

○ 26. SATURDAY / 27. SUNDAY

NOTES

January

Week 5

01/28/19 to 02/03/19

○ 28. MONDAY

○ 29. TUESDAY

○ 30. WEDNESDAY

○ 31. THURSDAY

○ 1. FRIDAY

○ 2. SATURDAY / 3. SUNDAY

NOTES

February

Week 6

02/04/19 to 02/10/19

○ 4. MONDAY

○ 5. TUESDAY

○ 6. WEDNESDAY

○ 7. THURSDAY

○ 8. FRIDAY

○ 9. SATURDAY / 10. SUNDAY

NOTES

February

Week 7

02/11/19 to 02/17/19

- [ ] 11. MONDAY

- [ ] 12. TUESDAY

- [ ] 13. WEDNESDAY

- [ ] 14. THURSDAY

- [ ] 15. FRIDAY

- [ ] 16. SATURDAY / 17. SUNDAY

NOTES

February

Week 8

02/18/19 to 02/24/19

- ◯ 18. MONDAY
- ◯ 19. TUESDAY
- ◯ 20. WEDNESDAY
- ◯ 21. THURSDAY
- ◯ 22. FRIDAY
- ◯ 23. SATURDAY / 24. SUNDAY

NOTES

February

Week 9

02/25/19 to 03/03/19

○ 25. MONDAY

○ 26. TUESDAY

○ 27. WEDNESDAY

○ 28. THURSDAY

○ 1. FRIDAY

○ 2. SATURDAY / 3. SUNDAY

NOTES

March

Week 10

03/04/19 to 03/10/19

○ 4. MONDAY

○ 5. TUESDAY

○ 6. WEDNESDAY

○ 7. THURSDAY

○ 8. FRIDAY

○ 9. SATURDAY / 10. SUNDAY

NOTES

March

Week 11

03/11/19 to 03/17/19

- ○ 11. MONDAY

- ○ 12. TUESDAY

- ○ 13. WEDNESDAY

- ○ 14. THURSDAY

- ○ 15. FRIDAY

- ○ 16. SATURDAY / 17. SUNDAY

NOTES

March

Week 12

03/18/19 to 03/24/19

- ○ 18. MONDAY

- ○ 19. TUESDAY

- ○ 20. WEDNESDAY

- ○ 21. THURSDAY

- ○ 22. FRIDAY

- ○ 23. SATURDAY / 24. SUNDAY

NOTES

March

Week 13

03/25/19 to 03/31/19

○ 25. MONDAY

○ 26. TUESDAY

○ 27. WEDNESDAY

○ 28. THURSDAY

○ 29. FRIDAY

○ 30. SATURDAY / 31. SUNDAY

NOTES

April

Week 14

04/01/19 to 04/07/19

- 1. MONDAY
- 2. TUESDAY
- 3. WEDNESDAY
- 4. THURSDAY
- 5. FRIDAY
- 6. SATURDAY / 7. SUNDAY

NOTES

April

Week 15

04/08/19 to 04/14/19

○ 8. MONDAY

○ 9. TUESDAY

○ 10. WEDNESDAY

○ 11. THURSDAY

○ 12. FRIDAY

○ 13. SATURDAY / 14. SUNDAY

NOTES

April

Week 16

04/15/19 to 04/21/19

○ 15. MONDAY

○ 16. TUESDAY

○ 17. WEDNESDAY

○ 18. THURSDAY

○ 19. FRIDAY

○ 20. SATURDAY / 21. SUNDAY

NOTES

April

Week 17

04/22/19 to 04/28/19

○ 22. MONDAY

○ 23. TUESDAY

○ 24. WEDNESDAY

○ 25. THURSDAY

○ 26. FRIDAY

○ 27. SATURDAY / 28. SUNDAY

NOTES

April

Week 18

04/29/19 to 05/05/19

○ 29. MONDAY

○ 30. TUESDAY

○ 1. WEDNESDAY

○ 2. THURSDAY

○ 3. FRIDAY

○ 4. SATURDAY / 5. SUNDAY

NOTES

May

Week 19

05/06/19 to 05/12/19

○ 6. MONDAY

○ 7. TUESDAY

○ 8. WEDNESDAY

○ 9. THURSDAY

○ 10. FRIDAY

○ 11. SATURDAY / 12. SUNDAY

NOTES

May

Week 20

05/13/19 to 05/19/19

○ 13. MONDAY

○ 14. TUESDAY

○ 15. WEDNESDAY

○ 16. THURSDAY

○ 17. FRIDAY

○ 18. SATURDAY / 19. SUNDAY

NOTES

May

Week 21

05/20/19 to 05/26/19

- 20. MONDAY

- 21. TUESDAY

- 22. WEDNESDAY

- 23. THURSDAY

- 24. FRIDAY

- 25. SATURDAY / 26. SUNDAY

NOTES

May

Week 22

05/27/19 to 06/02/19

○ 27. MONDAY

○ 28. TUESDAY

○ 29. WEDNESDAY

○ 30. THURSDAY

○ 31. FRIDAY

○ 1. SATURDAY / 2. SUNDAY

NOTES

June

Week 23

06/03/19 to 06/09/19

- ○ 3. MONDAY
- ○ 4. TUESDAY
- ○ 5. WEDNESDAY
- ○ 6. THURSDAY
- ○ 7. FRIDAY
- ○ 8. SATURDAY / 9. SUNDAY

NOTES

June

Week 24

06/10/19 to 06/16/19

○ 10. MONDAY

○ 11. TUESDAY

○ 12. WEDNESDAY

○ 13. THURSDAY

○ 14. FRIDAY

○ 15. SATURDAY / 16. SUNDAY

NOTES

June

Week 25

06/17/19 to 06/23/19

- ○ 17. MONDAY
- ○ 18. TUESDAY
- ○ 19. WEDNESDAY
- ○ 20. THURSDAY
- ○ 21. FRIDAY
- ○ 22. SATURDAY / 23. SUNDAY

NOTES

June

Week 26

06/24/19 to 06/30/19

○ 24. MONDAY

○ 25. TUESDAY

○ 26. WEDNESDAY

○ 27. THURSDAY

○ 28. FRIDAY

○ 29. SATURDAY / 30. SUNDAY

NOTES

July

Week 27

07/01/19 to 07/07/19

○ 1. MONDAY

○ 2. TUESDAY

○ 3. WEDNESDAY

○ 4. THURSDAY

○ 5. FRIDAY

○ 6. SATURDAY / 7. SUNDAY

NOTES

July

Week 28

07/08/19 to 07/14/19

○ 8. MONDAY

○ 9. TUESDAY

○ 10. WEDNESDAY

○ 11. THURSDAY

○ 12. FRIDAY

○ 13. SATURDAY / 14. SUNDAY

NOTES

July

Week 29

07/15/19 to 07/21/19

○ 15. MONDAY

○ 16. TUESDAY

○ 17. WEDNESDAY

○ 18. THURSDAY

○ 19. FRIDAY

○ 20. SATURDAY / 21. SUNDAY

NOTES

July

Week 30

07/22/19 to 07/28/19

○ 22. MONDAY

○ 23. TUESDAY

○ 24. WEDNESDAY

○ 25. THURSDAY

○ 26. FRIDAY

○ 27. SATURDAY / 28. SUNDAY

NOTES

July

Week 31

07/29/19 to 08/04/19

○ 29. MONDAY

○ 30. TUESDAY

○ 31. WEDNESDAY

○ 1. THURSDAY

○ 2. FRIDAY

○ 3. SATURDAY / 4. SUNDAY

NOTES

August

Week 32

08/05/19 to 08/11/19

○ 5. MONDAY

○ 6. TUESDAY

○ 7. WEDNESDAY

○ 8. THURSDAY

○ 9. FRIDAY

○ 10. SATURDAY / 11. SUNDAY

NOTES

August

Week 33

08/12/19 to 08/18/19

○ 12. MONDAY

○ 13. TUESDAY

○ 14. WEDNESDAY

○ 15. THURSDAY

○ 16. FRIDAY

○ 17. SATURDAY / 18. SUNDAY

NOTES

August

Week 34

08/19/19 to 08/25/19

○ 19. MONDAY

○ 20. TUESDAY

○ 21. WEDNESDAY

○ 22. THURSDAY

○ 23. FRIDAY

○ 24. SATURDAY / 25. SUNDAY

NOTES

August

Week 35

08/26/19 to 09/01/19

○ 26. MONDAY

○ 27. TUESDAY

○ 28. WEDNESDAY

○ 29. THURSDAY

○ 30. FRIDAY

○ 31. SATURDAY / 1. SUNDAY

NOTES

September

Week 36

09/02/19 to 09/08/19

○ 2. MONDAY

○ 3. TUESDAY

○ 4. WEDNESDAY

○ 5. THURSDAY

○ 6. FRIDAY

○ 7. SATURDAY / 8. SUNDAY

NOTES

September

Week 37

09/09/19 to 09/15/19

○ 9. MONDAY

○ 10. TUESDAY

○ 11. WEDNESDAY

○ 12. THURSDAY

○ 13. FRIDAY

○ 14. SATURDAY / 15. SUNDAY

NOTES

September

Week 38

09/16/19 to 09/22/19

○ 16. MONDAY

○ 17. TUESDAY

○ 18. WEDNESDAY

○ 19. THURSDAY

○ 20. FRIDAY

○ 21. SATURDAY / 22. SUNDAY

NOTES

September

Week 39

09/23/19 to 09/29/19

- ○ 23. MONDAY

- ○ 24. TUESDAY

- ○ 25. WEDNESDAY

- ○ 26. THURSDAY

- ○ 27. FRIDAY

- ○ 28. SATURDAY / 29. SUNDAY

NOTES

September

Week 40

09/30/19 to 10/06/19

○ 30. MONDAY

○ 1. TUESDAY

○ 2. WEDNESDAY

○ 3. THURSDAY

○ 4. FRIDAY

○ 5. SATURDAY / 6. SUNDAY

NOTES

October

Week 41

10/07/19 to 10/13/19

○ 7. MONDAY

○ 8. TUESDAY

○ 9. WEDNESDAY

○ 10. THURSDAY

○ 11. FRIDAY

○ 12. SATURDAY / 13. SUNDAY

NOTES

October

Week 42

10/14/19 to 10/20/19

○ 14. MONDAY

○ 15. TUESDAY

○ 16. WEDNESDAY

○ 17. THURSDAY

○ 18. FRIDAY

○ 19. SATURDAY / 20. SUNDAY

NOTES

October

Week 43

10/21/19 to 10/27/19

○ 21. MONDAY

○ 22. TUESDAY

○ 23. WEDNESDAY

○ 24. THURSDAY

○ 25. FRIDAY

○ 26. SATURDAY / 27. SUNDAY

NOTES

October

Week 44

10/28/19 to 11/03/19

○ 28. MONDAY

○ 29. TUESDAY

○ 30. WEDNESDAY

○ 31. THURSDAY

○ 1. FRIDAY

○ 2. SATURDAY / 3. SUNDAY

NOTES

November

Week 45

11/04/19 to 11/10/19

○ 4. MONDAY

○ 5. TUESDAY

○ 6. WEDNESDAY

○ 7. THURSDAY

○ 8. FRIDAY

○ 9. SATURDAY / 10. SUNDAY

NOTES

November

Week 46

11/11/19 to 11/17/19

○ 11. MONDAY

○ 12. TUESDAY

○ 13. WEDNESDAY

○ 14. THURSDAY

○ 15. FRIDAY

○ 16. SATURDAY / 17. SUNDAY

NOTES

November

Week 47

11/18/19 to 11/24/19

○ 18. MONDAY

○ 19. TUESDAY

○ 20. WEDNESDAY

○ 21. THURSDAY

○ 22. FRIDAY

○ 23. SATURDAY / 24. SUNDAY

NOTES

November

Week 48

11/25/19 to 12/01/19

○ 25. MONDAY

○ 26. TUESDAY

○ 27. WEDNESDAY

○ 28. THURSDAY

○ 29. FRIDAY

○ 30. SATURDAY / 1. SUNDAY

NOTES

December

Week 49

12/02/19 to 12/08/19

- ○ 2. MONDAY
- ○ 3. TUESDAY
- ○ 4. WEDNESDAY
- ○ 5. THURSDAY
- ○ 6. FRIDAY
- ○ 7. SATURDAY / 8. SUNDAY

NOTES

December

Week 50

12/09/19 to 12/15/19

○ 9. MONDAY

○ 10. TUESDAY

○ 11. WEDNESDAY

○ 12. THURSDAY

○ 13. FRIDAY

○ 14. SATURDAY / 15. SUNDAY

NOTES

December

Week 51

12/16/19 to 12/22/19

○ 16. MONDAY

○ 17. TUESDAY

○ 18. WEDNESDAY

○ 19. THURSDAY

○ 20. FRIDAY

○ 21. SATURDAY / 22. SUNDAY

NOTES

December

Week 52

12/23/19 to 12/29/19

○ 23. MONDAY

○ 24. TUESDAY

○ 25. WEDNESDAY

○ 26. THURSDAY

○ 27. FRIDAY

○ 28. SATURDAY / 29. SUNDAY

NOTES

December

Week 1

12/30/19 to 01/05/20

○ 30. MONDAY

○ 31. TUESDAY

○ 1. WEDNESDAY

○ 2. THURSDAY

○ 3. FRIDAY

○ 4. SATURDAY / 5. SUNDAY

NOTES

NOTES

NOTES

NOTES

NOTES

NOTES

NOTES

NOTES

NOTES

NOTES

NOTES

NOTES

NOTES

11348140R00076

Made in the USA
San Bernardino, CA
04 December 2018